BRITAIN IN OLD PHOTOGRAPHS

WALTHAM ABBEY

K.N. BASCOMBE

ALAN SUTTON PUBLISHING LIMITED

Alan Sutton Publishing Limited
Phoenix Mill · Far Thrupp · Stroud
Gloucestershire · GL5 2BU

First published 1995

Cover photographs: (front) the Church of the
Holy Cross and St Lawrence; (back) United
Dairies milkcart, 1932, on the road from
Waltham Cross to Waltham Abbey.

British Library Cataloguing in Publication Data.
A catalogue record for this book is available from
the British Library.

ISBN 0–7509–1029–1

Typeset in 9/10 Sabon.
Typesetting and origination by
Alan Sutton Publishing Limited.
Printed in Great Britain by
Ebenezer Baylis, Worcester.

Contents

Harold, last of the Saxon kings of England (1066), who built his church at Waltham.
The statue is in a niche at the south-west corner of the church.

Introduction

Waltham Abbey is a small market town in the south-west corner of Essex, lying on a gravel terrace between the River Lea and the rising ground of Epping Forest. The name Waltham is derived from 'weald' or 'wald', meaning a forest, and 'ham' indicating a Saxon homestead or settlement. As the result of a discovery in 1993 this early settlement is now thought to have been converted to Christianity by Mellitus, bishop of the East Saxons 604–16. The seventh-century church was of timber.

A stone church was subsequently built at Waltham, probably by the Mercian King Offa in about AD 790, and it was to this church that the Holy Cross was brought 240 years later by Tovi – a Danish nobleman. After Tovi's death Waltham reverted to King Edward the Confessor who granted it to Harold Godwinson, Earl of Wessex, who, for those fateful months in 1066, was King of England.

Harold is said to have been cured of a form of paralysis while praying before the Holy Cross of Waltham, and in gratitude he refounded the church in about 1060. His new church, an even grander stone building, has recently been identified through archaeological investigation. Harold's church was soon superseded by one in the more fashionable Norman or Romanesque style, and it is the nave of this which stands today. It was extended eastwards from 1177 as the monastic church, first as a priory and later as an abbey of Augustinian canons.

The dissolution of Waltham Abbey took place in 1540; it was the last of the monastic houses to be dissolved by Henry VIII. Despite an extensive inventory made at the time, no mention was made of the Holy Cross, and its fate remains a mystery to this day.

The right to hold a market was granted to the town by Richard I in 1189. The oldest surviving house dates from about 1400, and forms part of Lichgate House which adjoins the Welsh Harp inn in the Market Square. Few other medieval buildings survive, although the Epping Forest District Museum in Sun Street was originally a merchant's house and shop of 1520, and Nos 2, 3 and 4 Church Street have early sixteenth-century origins.

The water power of the River Lea gave rise to many industries, including cloth making, printing, flour milling, brewing, malting, pin making and calico and silk printing, but most importantly, the manufacture of gunpowder. This last had a great influence on the development of the town, and one section of this book is devoted to the Royal Gunpowder Factory.

Where do we find all this information? The history of a town and its people is derived from many sources. The people themselves remember their childhood and recall what their parents and grandparents told them. Records of various kinds can be found in many places: newspapers, church magazines, local histories and diaries, family bibles, census records and church registers. In the case of Waltham, church records go back to 1563 and the census records from 1841–91 are now available for study.

Maps too are indispensable for research into local history. The Tithe award maps of the early nineteenth century with lists of owners and occupiers of the land are an essential source. All of these can be found in the county record offices. At Waltham we are particularly fortunate to have access to a painted map of the town and adjoining land, dating from *c*. 1590, showing the streets we know today. Excavations by the Waltham Abbey Historical Society (WAHS) have shown that some of the lines on this map represent an enclosure called Eldeworth, first mentioned in 1235. This word means 'old enclosure'. Part of the line of this enclosure can be recognized as a property boundary today. Remains of vegetation found in the enclosure ditch were radio-carbon dated to *c*. 1250 BC, the time of the Middle Bronze Age. We cannot claim continuous occupation since that date, but evidence of a Roman presence has been discovered under the Market Square.

So from photographs, family and official records, the chance survival of early documents, archaeological excavation and the exercise of our imagination we have compiled this history of a town and its people.

THE TOWN OF
WALTHAM ABBEY

The development of the town was related to that of the church. Archaeological study suggests that the first church was established here in the seventh century on a royal estate. A local community would have grown up, round which developed the town. The written word begins with the *de Inventione Sancte Crucis* (concerning the discovery of the Holy Cross), written about 1180. This tells how Tovi, one of King Cnut's leading ministers, was building a lowly hut at Waltham and how, *c.* 1030, he brought here a black marble cross, bearing a figure of Christ, from Montacute in Somerset. King Harold prayed before it on his way to the battle of Hastings in 1066 when the figure on the cross bowed its head. After the Conquest, the town grew and was granted charters for a market and annual fairs. Royal visits were frequent until the Abbey was dissolved in 1540.

The story since has been one of a country town, not very prosperous, whose principal industry was gunpowder manufacture. In the twentieth century, proximity to London has resulted in a great increase in size. Waltham is near the centre of the Lee Valley Regional Park. Note that the River Lea is spelt Lee in official documents, following its use in the title of the Regional Park.

The Old Market House. This building was erected in the Market Square in about 1670 and demolished in 1852. It superseded an earlier Moot Hall. This prominent site was also probably that of the Anglo-Saxon moot where justice was dispensed. Roman evidence was found deep below the present level.

𝔓roclamation *of Richard II, issued at Waltham Abbey, June 23rd, 1381 to the delegates of the Essex Rebels. (Peasants' Revolt).*

O MISERABLE men, hateful by land and sea, not worthy even to live, you ask to be equal with your lords. You would most certainly have suffered the vilest death, if We had not resolved to observe our pledges to your messengers. But since you have come in the role of messengers, you shall not die forthwith, but shall enjoy your lives, in order that you may truly relate Our answer to your fellows. Therefore carry to your colleagues this answer on the part of the King. "Serfs you have been, and are; and you shall remain in bondage, not as hitherto, but incomparably more vile. For so long as, by the grace of God, We live and reign in this Kingdom, We shall use Our sense, Our strength, and Our property so to treat you, that your slavery shall serve as an example to those who come after you, and that those now living and those to come who resemble yourselves, may have your wretchedness always before their eyes, as it were in a mirror, and shall have reason to curse you, and fear of doing such things as you have done." As for yourselves, who have come as messengers, your mission and your duty being fulfilled, you shall live your lives, if you will decide to adhere to Us and so to continue faithfully and loyally. Now, therefore, judge for yourselves which is the better, when you return to your fellows with your mission completed.

This text of the Proclamation of Richard II, in response to the Peasants' Revolt, is translated from the Latin of Thomas of Walsingham, a fifteenth-century monk of St Albans.

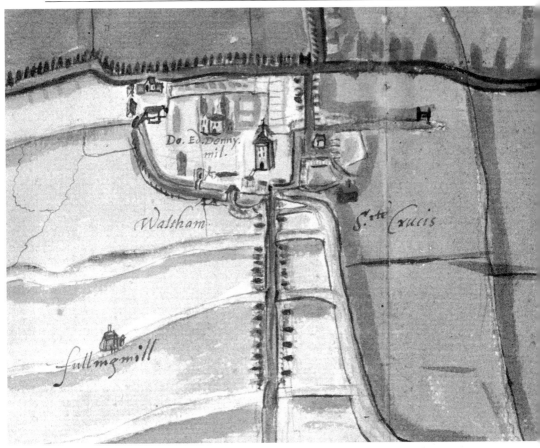

The oldest map of Waltham, *c.* 1594, with east at the top. It is part of a larger map now in the Hatfield House library. The lord of the manor, Edward Denny, built the house shown (see p. 65). Very few Abbey buildings remain fifty years after the Dissolution. Those at the top left are part of the monastic farm of Waltham Grange. The Moot Hall can be seen in the Market Place. The road layout is still recognizable today.

The market in the 1930s. The Lichgate House, with the church behind, can be seen in the background.

Market day viewed from the church tower, *c.* 1970. The Lichgate House, bottom centre, was originally a priest's house. Upton's shoe shop, across the road, houses the oldest family business in Essex; it was founded in 1777 (see p. 62).

The post office and Greyhound Inn, *c.* 1920. In the late seventeenth century the inn included the two buildings further left, and the entrance to the inn yard was through the opening at the end of the range.

Sun Street from the east. This was probably taken before the First World War, and shows the Geisha Tea Rooms (left) and the New Inn (right).

A painting of Bakers Entry, by Thomas Shotter Boys (1803–74), looking south from the church, *c*. 1830. Excavations in 1976 showed a sequence of five bread ovens dating from *c*. 1200 into the seventeenth century.

A general view of Sun Street from the west, *c*. 1910.

This ancient elm in the churchyard was a well-known landmark; it was bound together with an iron strap in 1859 and survived until 1983, when it was replaced by a tulip tree.

Milk delivery, 1920s. All deliveries at this time were made by horse and cart. The churn from which the milk was measured into the customer's jug can be seen. This milk-cart is driven by 'Pop' Warren.

Buildings of *c*. 1735, demolished in 1891, which stood in front of the Vicarage. They belonged to the water mill, the miller living in the house on the right.

The Vicarage, recently the Rectory, as seen today. There is documentary evidence for a date of about 1630 and the projecting wing may be of that period.

The National School, *c.* 1890. In spite of criticism from the church authorities the school was demolished in 1902 as the site was needed for the new town hall (see opposite).

Other buildings demolished to make way for the new town hall. The small building (left) housed the horse-drawn fire engine. Next door were the police station, a reading room and magistrates' rooms. The first meeting of the Waltham Abbey Building Society was held here in 1847. The gabled building was the first Leverton School (see p. 18).

The late John Bentley standing outside the town hall built by his great-grandfather, also John Bentley. This striking building is one of the very few art nouveau town halls in the country.

The Leverton School moved here to Greenyard. The school was founded in 1823 (see p. 16) under the will of Thomas Leverton, a leading architect of his day. It was administered by the Leverton Charity until the 1940s. Mrs Gladys Bird was one of the last teachers to work there.

The Baptist Church in Paradise Row. There has been a Baptist chapel on this site since 1729. This present church was built in 1836 and including 'Vestries, Schools and other appendages' cost £1,320.

Camp's Court, *c.* 1887. The lad fishing is standing on the south side of the Cornmill tail stream; the church is seen to the north-east. The gable with the chimney is the end of a row of cottages forming part of a notorious slum called Camp's Court after its builder.

Oak panelling. This dates from about 1530 and was almost certainly made for the last abbot, Robert Fuller. It includes the portcullis, the emblem of Henry VIII, and the pomegranate of Catherine of Aragon. At the Dissolution it was incorporated by Anthony Denny into the Abbey House (see p. 65); when that was demolished in 1770 it was placed in an old house in Greenyard; in 1899 it was purchased by the Victoria & Albert Museum.

Detail of the oak panelling. Part of this panelling can be seen in the Epping Forest District Museum at 41 Sun Street, where it has been used to panel a whole room.

The house on the east side of Greenyard in which the oak panelling was installed; it was removed just before the building was gutted by fire. The doctor's surgery now stands here. The cottages on the right survive today.

The east side of Sewardstone Street, early twentieth century. The dilapidated house was demolished in the 1920s and the site was excavated in 1966. It was owned by Thomas Winspear, a London merchant, in the seventeenth century; some of his tableware, including a beautiful Turkish Isnik plate, was found in a cesspit.

The west side of Sewardstone Street. The jettied weather-boarded house is of seventeenth-century date.

Nobel's factory in Farm Hill Road. From about 1910 till 1936 cartridge cases were made here. It was sold to Messrs Catalin Ltd who manufactured plastics. One of their products, a cast phenolic resin, was used in the science of photoelasticity; this is a method of assessing stresses in models of engineering structures and components.

The interior of Nobel's factory during the First World War.

These nineteenth-century cottages on the south side of Highbridge Street were Royal Gunpowder factory workmen's quarters. By 1892 they were in a state of disrepair and the site became the grounds of a new residence for the superintendent of the factory, called Government House, which stood till 1980.

Jonah and the Whale. During the 1892 demolition of the superintendent's house, which adjoined the above cottages to the east, this tempera painting was discovered. It is now in the Museum of London.

A delightful picture taken in about 1891. The boat appears to be tied up fore and aft! This is a picture looking north, on the River Lea itself, at the back of cottages on the south side of Highbridge Street; on the left are the outbuildings of the superintendent's house. This well-dressed group might be the superintendent's family.

Two views looking east along Highbridge Street. Notice the difference in the church tower; the upper part was rebuilt in 1904. The top picture of *c.* 1890 shows the narrow approach to the church caused by the presence of the miller's house. The lower picture of *c.* 1910 shows the Capital and Counties Bank, now the Midland, and the recently renamed Old Court House, once the YWCA, which face each other across the street. The church clock was donated by John Parnell to commemorate the Golden Jubilee of 1897.

Highbridge Street, c. 1890. The county court of 1848 is on the left; the almshouses, founded by Francis Greene in 1626 and rebuilt in 1818, and the Ordnance Arms are on the right.

A barge unloading timber from Mile End at Waltham Lock on the River Lee Navigation some time before 1924. In that year the water level under Station Road (the western extension of Highbridge Street) was lowered by transferring the lock to the north side of it.

The Romeland, from roomland, meaning open space. On this west side, the jetties, gables and attics of *c.* 1650 are interspersed with smaller later houses. At the left is part of Reformation House, built in about 1725 for Richard Hitchin, a butcher.

Houses along the north of Romeland. The centre group has a façade of *c.* 1700. Note the cattle pens; a market was held here until about 1975. The 165 ft deep well in the centre was dug in 1877.

The east side of Romeland including The Crown public house of *c*. 1790. Most of the buildings around Romeland were destroyed by a parachute mine which dropped just to the north. These on the east side survived. The gabled façade beyond belonged to a pin factory erected in 1792. The business closed in about 1850. Excavations by Waltham Abbey Historical Society in 1973/4 showed that under Reformation House there were remains of a late fifteenth-century 'screens-passage' house probably owned by Henry VIII, to which he may have resorted with Anne Boleyn when he was still married to Catherine of Aragon. Besides many jetons, coin-like objects used for counting in Roman numerals, there was a collection of glass bottles probably belonging to Richard Hitchin, and numerous small Victorian objects which had fallen between the floorboards.

East end of Sun Street, *c.* 1950. This shows the Wesleyan Church built in 1902 by Walter Lawrence; he also built Nobel's factory (see p. 23). In the mid-1970s a new Methodist church was opened in Farm Hill Road and this building became the Catholic church.

Sun Street looking west. In 1981 Sun Street was pedestrianized and the bus service had to be re-routed. The lady on the left is standing outside the Epping Forest District Museum at No. 41.

Read all about it! The closure of Sun Street to vehicles is forecast. On the left is the police station, which opened in 18/6.

Taylor's travelling show. Early in the twentieth century many such shows made regular visits to the town. Taylor's stood supreme. Each performance ended with a display of 'electric fireworks'. Over 1,000 coloured lamps were used, fading into one another and harmonizing with music from the organ. The increasing popularity of cinema caused the end of these shows.

The Board, later Council, School. It was built in 1874 on open ground to the south of Sun Street, and was used for over ninety years.

Section Two

THE CHURCH OF THE HOLY CROSS AND ST LAWRENCE

The first church on this site was of timber. The second was of stone, and is believed to have been built by King Offa of the Mercians in about 790 AD. The third church, built by Harold, was dedicated *c.* 1060. Then the Norman or Romanesque church, built from *c.* 1090 to *c.* 1150, the nave of which serves as the present church, was the fourth. The fifth was the Augustinian monastic church started in 1177 and dedicated in 1242.

As part of his penance after the murder of Thomas à Becket, Henry II, in 1177, began to construct the monastic buildings on the east end of the fourth church. This resulted in a combined church about 500 ft (150m) long with two crossings; the western part served as the parish church, probably dedicated to St Lawrence, while the main altar of the monastic part was probably dedicated to the Holy Cross. The twelve secular canons of Harold's foundation were ejected in favour of eighteen Augustinian canons.

At the Dissolution of the Monasteries there was a suggestion that the Abbey would become a cathedral. This did not come about, probably because it was too near London and was not central to Essex.

The building which now serves as the parish church is a place of great beauty; people have worshipped here for over a thousand years.

The Abbey gateway, built in 1369. Only part remains, but it would have been similar in size to the gateway at St Albans. This was the main entrance over the Cornmill stream into the Abbey precinct. The church tower seen here was built by the parishioners in the sixteenth century to house the bells; these were originally in the crossing tower at the other end of the church. Part of the pin factory (see p. 29) can be seen on the right.

Pilgrim's badge sold to visitors to the shrine of the Holy Cross. The Latin inscription reads 'Sign of the Holy Cross of Waltham'. This example was cast from a stone mould found in the city of London in the nineteenth century.

The eleventh-century seal of the Holy Cross of Waltham. One side shows two heads, believed to be of Harold and Tovi, and is inscribed in Latin, 'By this charter Harold confirms a grant with Tovi.'

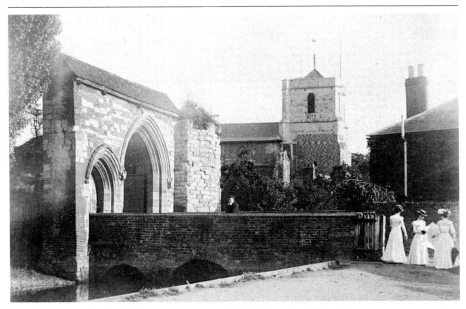

Another view of the Abbey gateway, *c.* 1895. Note the Victorian costumes complete with parasols.

The water-powered flour mill, demolished in 1907, viewed from near the Abbey gateway. The races and bearing housings for the two mill wheels remain; the sluices can still be operated.

Miss E.M. Hawthorne, church caretaker in the 1920s and '30s, stands at the south door of the church. The door and most of the doorway were renewed in the 1859–60 restoration by William Burges. The inner columns and the carving at the top (see p. 49) are original twelfth-century work.

This print of 1819 shows the church with the Denny family mausoleum at the right. This was built in about 1635 and removed in about 1821. The church roof and parapet at the east end are original. The rest of the roof was reduced in pitch in 1807; some of the twelfth-century timbers remain.

An earlier print of 1771 shows the tower with an embattled top and stair turret, and the roof at its original pitch. The long building on the right is the watermill.

This fine but mutilated statue of the Madonna was found in 1974 carefully buried in a ditch on the north side of Sun Street. Made from Reigate stone, it is dated *c.* 1380 by her costume. Note the buttons on the sleeve and on the front of the sideless gown. This may be the statue of the Guild of Our Lady. It can be seen in the crypt.

Archaeology in progress. Left, Mary Salton and the late Joe Smith examine the wall of the monastic sewer. The picture below shows excavation of a building in 1970; probably a day house for monastic workers, it was a timber-framed structure which sat on the ground walls seen. It was situated in Veresmead and is now under the Abbey View bypass. In the distance is Peter Huggins who has directed Waltham Abbey Historical Society excavations here since 1966.

The marked site of the burial of King Harold. After the battle of Hastings it is said that Edith Swan-neck pleaded with Duke William to be allowed to bring back the body of Harold for burial. On the anniversary of the battle, 14 October, a wreath is laid on the grave by WAHS and a ceremony is staged by the English Companions.

Following excavations of 1987–91 further west it is now known that this marker stone does not lie within the walls of Harold's church. Rather, he would have been buried in the continuous transept or nave of his own church (see the model on p. 43). When the Romanesque church was built the body may have been moved into the choir of the building, but the tomb is still likely to be west of this marker.

The signatures of the Abbot and Canons of Waltham on the Deed of Surrender of the Augustinian monastery in 1540. Below is the signature of William Petre, the King's Commissioner.

Queen Mary, widow of King George V, walks down the churchyard path with the vicar, the Revd A.V.G. Cleall, 1938.

A model of Harold's church of *c.* 1060 made by members of Waltham Abbey Historical Society. The plan is based on results of excavations from 1985–91, the elevations on research into other contemporary buildings. This is the church, the fourth on the site, in which Harold would have been buried in 1066 (see p. 41).

Internal view of the Romanesque church looking east. The east end is the work of William Burges (1860) with stained glass designed by Edward Burne-Jones. The ceiling panels were painted by Edward Poynter, *c.* 1862. The pillars are similar to those at Durham and masons from there may have worked here at Waltham.

A close-up of the centre of the east end. The beautiful stone reredos, designed by William Burges in 1876, was carved by Thomas Nichols; it depicts the story of the Nativity and the flight into Egypt. The altar, made of American black walnut, dates from 1873. Both were donated by Mrs Edenborough.

The Lady Chapel, built *c.* 1350. It is thought that this was built, not as a lady chapel, which would have been further east, but as the chapel of a funeral guild, the Guild of God and St Mary. The undercroft or crypt below was a chapel dedicated to St Sepulchre. It was called the Charnel, and used to house the bones of guild members. The wall painting above the altar, dating from *c.* 1400, represents the Last Judgement, appropriate for the chapel of a charnel guild; discovered in the 1870s, it has been restored twice, in 1931 and in 1968.

The view from the Lady Chapel towards the altar.

Detail of the wall painting after the 1968 restoration. Here we see St Peter, recognized by the crossed keys, welcoming a bishop or abbot into the New Jerusalem.

King Henry II, 1154–89. Henry was the first Plantagenet King of England and much of France, and laid the basis of the English jury system. He is chiefly remembered today for his quarrel with his one-time friend Thomas à Becket, who was murdered in Canterbury Cathedral by those believing they were acting on Henry's orders.

Grotesque masks allowed the mason to demonstrate his skills. Such heads can be seen inside, at gallery level, as corbels supporting attached shafts, and outside, at roof level, in the eastern two bays supporting the parapet.

Close-up of the capitals of the east jamb of the south door of *c*. 1120. The inner capital has a pair of beasts with strap-work ornament. The beasts show Viking influence, but remember the Normans were Vikings who had settled in northern France.

Early fourteenth-century glazed floor tiles. These were found in 1969 in a doorway of the abbot's private quarters. They are attributed to the itinerant 'Westminster tiler', so named because there are similar tiles at Westminster Abbey.

This carved head forms the terminal of a hood mould over the west door of the south aisle. A document of 1286 calls on the people to repair this end of the church, and the west front must date from this time.

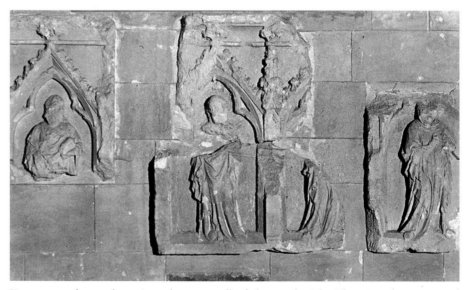

Fragments of a tomb set into the east wall of the south aisle. They may be associated with a Purbeck marble head now in the museum at 41 Sun Street and may be part of the tomb of Sir Richard le Brus, *c*. 1244–86, an uncle of Robert the Bruce of Scotland. These fragments are also known as 'The Weepers'.

The Denny tomb in the south aisle, the finest monument in the church. This is Sir Edward Denny who died in 1600 while campaigning in Ireland; he was a grandson of Sir Anthony who leased the abbey lands of Waltham from Henry VIII. He is shown in armour while his wife, Margaret Edgecombe, is in ruff, hood and stomacher, although she is buried in Bishop's Stortford. Note the ten children below, one being led by the hand.

Thomas Tallis, organist at Waltham at the time of the Dissolution in 1540. He is sometimes described as the father of church music. In 1575 he and William Byrd were granted a monopoly in music printing. In 1540 he became a Gentleman of the Chapel Royal, a post which he held till his death in 1589. Many of Tallis' compositions are in current use as hymn tunes. The best known is 'Tallis' Canon', to which is usually sung 'Glory to Thee, my God, this night'.

Example of music by Tallis. Note the five-line stave already in use.

The 'Ringers Window', which was located in the tower over the west door, was destroyed by enemy action. The design was by William Burges and it commemorated the Revd James Francis, vicar of this parish for forty years, who died in 1885, and his brother Edward who died in 1878.

Aries, one of the signs of the zodiac painted on canvas ceiling panels by Edward Poynter in 1862. Also depicted are the labours of the months, the four elements and past and present.

INNS AND SHOPS

In towns all over the country, where farmers and traders gathered for weekly markets, there were many hostelries. Waltham Abbey was no exception. With the decline of the town as a market centre, many of the public houses have closed, and most of those that remain have changed their character and now provide a wide variety of food, catering increasingly for the general public and for visitors.

Until the middle of the twentieth century the three main shopping areas, Highbridge Street, Market Place and Sun Street, were lined almost exclusively with small family businesses; some passed from father to son for several generations. In the 1886 *Kelly's Directory* of Essex over thirty different tradesmen and shops are listed in the town. They range from baker, beer retailer, boot maker, brewer, builder and butcher to watchmaker and wheelwright. No doubt all the day-to-day needs of the community would have been satisfied locally.

Only a few of the inns and shops shown in this section are still trading. Supermarkets have been built within easy reach, private transport has become more readily available and the shopping habits of the population have consequently changed.

The 'Telegraph' coach outside the Welsh Harp, which is situated along the north side of the Market Square, *c.* 1900. The word 'Welsh' is said to derive from the Welsh troops billeted there during the Napoleonic wars of 1793–1815. Certainly a document of 1740 refers just to The Harp. The sign is probably that of Pryor, Reid and Co. Ltd; later photographs show it as the Watney, Combe and Reid Brewery.

The Welsh Harp early in the twentieth century before the timbers were exposed. Notice the brewery sign differs from the previous page, but this picture must have been taken before 1904 as the church tower in the background has yet to be altered.

The White Horse at the north-east corner of the Market Square, replaced in about 1960 by an unattractive Barclays Bank designed by a local architect. Note the soldiers of the First World War, some on bicycles and some on horseback.

The trade card of S. Pugh, linen draper and haberdasher, whose premises were at 24 Sun Street in 1902. Mr Pugh appears to have stocked a wide variety of goods. In 1896 the business was known as Pugh and Richards.

The Baker's Arms, built in about 1840, at the entrance to Romeland. It was demolished in about 1975 when the area was redeveloped after the closure of the cattle market. Buildings to the right and left remain today.

Webb's, family butchers, of 40 Highbridge Street, *c.* 1900. Their trade card stated 'Purveyors of dairy fed pork and home-made sausages, all meat of the best quality. Families waited on daily.' Today's refrigerated environment calls into question the standard of hygiene, with the meat hanging outside.

Arthur Summers, saddler and harness maker, outside his shop at 9 Sun Street, *c.* 1920. The shop dates from 1827, as recorded on the rain-water head.

The Ordnance Arms in Highbridge Street (see p. 27) was completely destroyed by a V2 rocket in March 1945. One of the few items rescued from the ruins was a box of dominoes; the box was intact but, alas, several dominoes were missing.

Mr Sharp's fish shop was demolished in 1962 when the needs of traffic were considered paramount, and a new row of shops was built behind. The Green Dragon (on the right) is part of the west side of the Market Square which dates from *c.* 1570; its existence as a public house has been traced back to 1800.

The staff at the Honey Lane post office at the corner of Eastbrook Road, *c.* 1904. Probably built in 1890, the post office was still serving the public in 1929.

The gentleman standing in the doorway with such a proprietary air must surely be the owner of this general store. Neither has been identified.

Upton's boot makers at the north-west corner of the Market Place; part of the *c.* 1570 range of buildings. The lady is probably Mrs Elizabeth Upton, who died in 1916; she was the daughter-in-law of Jesse Upton, an eccentric inclined to poetry. The business was moved here by Jesse from Sun Street in 1872 (see p. 11).

Highbridge Street looking west, 1911. Miss Mabel Gayler ran the family newsagent's business until the Second World War. The cart in the background and the new motor car show contrasting means of transport.

PERSONALITIES

At the Domesday survey of 1086 there were 150 men in the whole manor of Waltham, indicating a total population of under 700 people, with fewer than 200 houses. By 1235 this had grown to 250 houses and by 1662 to 320, the gradual growth being dependent on what the land could support. By 1801 the population was 3,040, by 1901 it was 6,549 and by 1961 it had grown to 10,958.

There were many reasons for the rapid growth in the first half of the twentieth century: principally the improvement in transport to and from London, the development of small local industries and the increase in size of the Royal Gunpowder Factory.

In this section we show some of the people who live, or have lived, in Waltham.

Sir Anthony Denny, 1501–49, was educated at St Paul's School, London, and St John's College, Cambridge, and in about 1520 entered diplomatic service. By 1535 he had won the confidence of Henry VIII and in 1547 was the only person who dared tell the king he was dying – technically an act of treason. He became a privy councillor in 1538 and in 1541, a year after the Dissolution of the Monasteries, he was granted a lease of part of the land surrounding the Abbey. In 1537 he acquired the site of Cheshunt Nunnery.

Abbey House, which stood in what is now the Abbey gardens, was built by Sir Edward Denny using residual materials from the dismantling of the monastery. The pair of gateposts on the left and the remains of fireplaces and windows visible today indicate its position. The two projecting wings in this view date from c. 1690, and the central façade from c. 1730. The building was pulled down in 1770, possibly after a fire.

The fame of Henry Bridges rests on one achievement only, the construction in about 1734 of an elaborate monumental clock called the Microcosm. In 1741 it was on view at the Mitre near Charing Cross, and was purchased by Edward Davis. In 1756 it was exhibited in America, after which nothing is known of it until it was recognized in Paris after the First World War and bought by the British Museum.

The Microcosm. Apart from a great deal of astronomical data, the moving parts included ships, coaches, carts, horses, a windmill, various animals, a gunpowder mill with a flow of water, workmen, maids, a carpenter's yard and two boys playing see-saw!

The monument, in Waltham Abbey churchyard, to Henry Bridges, who died in 1754.

An illustration from the *Book of Martyrs* by John Foxe, showing the death of thirteen martyrs who were burnt at Stratford, London, on 27 June 1556, because they would not recant their Protestant faith; one of these was William Halliwell, a smith of Waltham.

John Foxe was educated at Magdalen College, Oxford, and became a fellow in 1539. He resigned in 1545 as his conscience would not accept some of the college statutes. He left England for the continent in 1553 when the anti-Protestant Queen Mary came to the throne. He returned in 1559 and the first English edition of his book was published in 1562–3. Foxe and his family came to live in Waltham in 1564. He died in 1587 and was buried at St Giles, Cripplegate.

Thomas Fuller DD, 1608–61, was a church historian who came to Waltham as chaplain to James Hay, Earl of Carlisle, who presented him to the perpetual curacy of Waltham in 1648. He is perhaps best known for his *Church History of Britain*. Among his other writings was a history of Waltham Abbey, the first history of an Essex parish to be published.

A Salvation Army sewing circle in the early twentieth century; note the sewing machine. Included in this picture are Mrs Pegrum, Mrs Sally Baines, Mrs Johnson, Mrs Kate Wren, Mrs F. Ledger, Mrs Rodgers, Mrs Watts, Mrs Appleton, Mrs Webb, Mrs Waller and Beatty Conyard. The Salvation Army Citadel in Sewardstone Street was opened in 1908.

Two Salvation Army Bands. The first, of c. 1920, includes two young cornet players, probably members of the junior band. The second shows the band in 1960 playing in the Abbey Church under the direction of 'Bill' Jackson.

A very early picture of the Waltham Abbey Scout Band.

The military band of the Essex Yeomanry, c. 1912. The double bass player on the extreme right changed his instrument for a tuba when on the march, for obvious reasons!

David Carter, 1809–93, with his wife Sarah (née Skinner) and family, c. 1860. He was the owner of a greengrocer's shop in Highbridge Street opposite the Romeland. He also owned a market garden and orchard on land now known as Cartersfield estate. The elder son is Thomas (see below).

Thomas Carter, 1849–1931, and his wife Caroline (née Bentley), with their children Edward, Frank, Donald, Janet and David, c. 1894. Thomas was also a market gardener.

Edward Carter, 1872–1919, with his wife Phoebe (née Ward) and children Jessie and Edward John, 1905.

This house in Sewardstone Street, built in 1760, was the Carter family home for nearly a hundred years. The house, market garden and orchard were later owned by Mr William Brooker, hence nearby Brooker Road and Orchard Gardens.

Mrs Rose Puddephatt seated on her husband's motor bike, early 1920s. The lady in the side-car is thought to be her mother. Notice the carbide lamps on the handlebars and the sidecar, and bulb horn.

Sidney Puddephatt, her husband, carried on a haberdashery business previously owned by his father at 6 Sun Street. Sidney had a great interest in local history, was a founder member of the Waltham Abbey Historical Society and started the collection of photographs from which most of the pictures in this book have been selected.

Sidney Puddephatt, on the left, seen with Sir Hereward Wake, September 1964. Sir Hereward is the Lord of the Manor of Waltham, and resides at Courteenhall, the Wake family home in Northamptonshire.

John Bentley, who built the Waltham Abbey town hall in 1904 (see p. 17). He also built housing in Rue de St Lawrence and Foxe's Parade, Waltham Abbey, and constructed the churches of St James, Freezywater, and St Thomas, Upshire. Members of the Bentley family lived for many years at 39 and 41 Sun Street, now the Epping Forest District Museum.

This picture is said to show Macedonian gypsies in Epping Forest. Possibly they were charcoal burners.

Five members of the Turnham family, all of whom were employed as coopers in the Royal Gunpowder Factory in the early twentieth century.

An unknown group arranged on the steps at the rear of Joyce House, Farm Hill Road.

A group of Abbey Church workers, c. 1922. They are gathered around the vicar, the Revd Francis Burdett Johnston and the curate, the Revd Ambrose Bell; between them is Mrs Rose Bell. Also shown are Miss Hawthorne (p. 37), Miss Mabel Gayler (p. 62), Edward Carter (p. 75), Miss Helen Marshall, Miss Alps, Francis Hale, Miss Fanny Sapsford (vicar's housekeeper), Kathleen Carter and Grace Conyard.

Children at a private day school run at 8 Sun Street by the Misses Eversfield, 1890. Three girls and a small boy have identical lace collars.

A fund-raising meeting of the YWCA at St Kilda's, Highbridge Street (see p. 26), early twentieth century. The Revd Gifford H. Johnson, local historian and formerly curate of Waltham Abbey, and Stevenson Cox, editor of the Waltham Abbey *Weekly Telegraph*, are seen at the rear. What marvellous hats!

A procession of dignitaries, including the lord lieutenant of Essex, approaching the town hall after a ceremony in the church.

A yard off Sewardstone Street where Len Platt (left) carried on a cycle repair business; also in the picture are plumber Bill Pickett and coalman Alf Gaywood. The building was gutted by fire in 1953.

Bert Gladwin, one of the council's outside staff, pictured in the Market Square, early 1970s. He was a familiar sight around the town centre.

WALTHAM AT WAR

The first picture relates to the First World War between the Allies and the Central Powers which lasted from August 1914 to November 1918. The other pictures are of the Second World War. It was on 3 September 1939 that the prime minister, Neville Chamberlain, told the nation that we were again at war with Germany. This lasted, on the British front in North Germany, until 4 May 1945 when the German command surrendered at the headquarters of Field Marshal Montgomery on Luneberg Heath near Hanover. The final surrender in the west was to the supreme commander, General Eisenhower, on 7 May at Rheims.

In the Second World War Waltham was on the receiving end of 499 bombs of various sizes, 15 parachute mines, 14 V1 doodlebugs or bombs propelled by a ramjet engine, 16 V2 rockets and 30 containers of incendiary bombs. In spite of this bombardment Waltham suffered only seven fatal casualties. The town had the dubious honour of receiving the last doodlebug to fall in the London region, which fell at Claverhambury on 28 March 1945. It was very nearly the last in England, but one more fell next day.

The west end of Church Street, 1914. The Essex Yeomanry are about to depart for the Western Front. The building with the pediment was built in 1845 for worship on Strict and Particular Baptist principles and was called Bethel. Worship ceased there between 1906 and 1912 and the building became the local headquarters of the Essex Yeomanry.

Waltham Abbey Fire Brigade in front of the town hall during the Second World War. Blast walls protect the ground floor.

The Air Raid Precautions carnival float, probably in 1939. The inscription is self-explanatory.

Evacuation rehearsal in Greenfield Street. In anticipation of air attacks on the Royal Gunpowder Factory, and consequent bombing in the town, evacuation practices were held in the early days of the war. On the left is John Carter with his mother Mary.

The unexploded bomb recovered here by the Bomb Disposal Squad is a 1,000 kg Hermann which fell at Pynest Green on 16 August 1942.

This is the combustion chamber and expansion nozzle of a V2 rocket which fell in Epping Forest on 20 November 1944. The warden approaching it rather gingerly is Mick Smith.

A V2 rocket fell in Highbridge Street on 7 March 1945. This was Waltham's most serious incident. The crater, which soon filled with water from severed water mains, reached right across the road. Gas mains and telephone cables were shattered and the sewage pumping system was affected. The county court, the almshouses (see p. 27) and several other houses were wrecked, while other buildings including the Ordnance Arms (see p. 60) were completely destroyed. There were four deaths and fifty-three people injured.

The V2 had a liquid-propelled rocket motor using a mixture of ethyl alcohol and water as fuel and liquid oxygen as oxidant. The motor consisted of a turbine-driven pumping system operated by concentrated hydrogen peroxide which delivered the main propellants to the combustion chamber (see p. 86).

The control point for the Highbridge Street incident was set up and manned by wardens Joe Parsley, Archie Clark and Mick Smith.

The scene of devastation in Highbridge Street, looking west towards the almshouses. Notice the water-filled crater. The V2 rockets often exploded when the propellants were exhausted, with the warhead travelling on alone. This must have happened in this case, as the combustion chamber was found at Skillethill Farm, Honey Lane, about a mile and a half away.

THE ROYAL GUNPOWDER FACTORY

Gunpowder manufacture at Waltham can be traced back to the 1660s, when a former oil mill was converted to a powder mill. The constituents of gunpowder are saltpetre, sulphur and charcoal, and a large number of powder mills are recorded down the Lea, but all except Waltham, the furthest upstream, ceased working by 1700. The fact that Waltham controlled its own water supply may have been the reason for its survival. A print of 1735 shows horse mills, dumb mills, stamping mills and a corning and glazing engine, the latter two clearly shown with water wheels. In 1787 the government considered it desirable to buy the works. Major Congreve, deputy controller of the Royal Laboratory at Woolwich, agreed and the purchase was effected. The mills were thus ready to meet the needs of the Napoleonic wars with France.

In 1872 a guncotton factory was built; guncotton is formed by treating cellulose such as cotton with acids. In 1891 the first cordite, a mixture of nitrocellulose and nitroglycerine, was made here. Cordite became the standard explosive of the British Army. The factory closed in 1945. The site then became the government Explosive, Research and Development Establishment (ERDE).

The Congreve rocket was invented in 1805 and used by the British, in a massed attack, at the battle of Copenhagen in 1807 when the city was set on fire. The rocket could be launched at sea as shown here. Congreve (see opposite) carried out some of his researches at Waltham and wrote pamphlets about his work. In 1828 he had to flee the country after some shady dealings, and died in Toulouse. It is ironic that one of the last V2 rockets fell less than a quarter of a mile from where Congreve worked (see p. 87).

Major William Congreve, Bt, 1772–1828, with a carriage for the land launching of his rocket and a representation of the burning Copenhagen in the background.

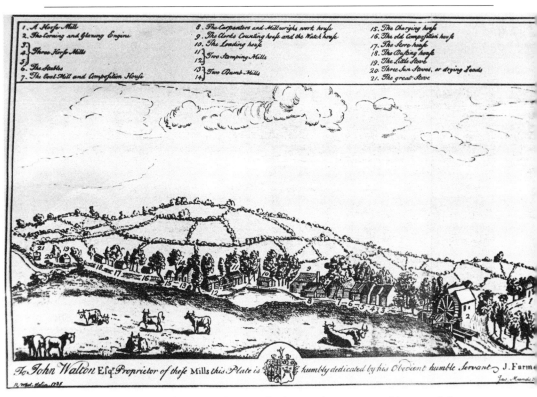

1. A Horse Mill
2. The Corning and Glazing Engine
3.
4. Three Horse Mills
5.
6. The Stables
7. The Coal Mill and Composition House

8. The Carpenters and Millwrights work house
9. The Clerks Counting house and the Watch house
10. The Loading house
11. Two Stamping Mills
12.
13. Two Dumb Mills
14.

15. The Charging house
16. The old Composition house
17. The Seve house
18. The Dusting house
19. The Little Stove
20. Three Sun Stoves, or drying Leads
21. The great Stove

To John Walton Esqr. Proprietor of these Mills this Plate is humbly dedicated by his Obedient humble Servant J. Farmer

A view from the west of the Waltham mills from John Farmer's history of the town, 1735. The dependence of the works on water, both for turning the mill wheels and for navigation of the powder barges, is shown.

An important part of gunpowder manufacture was the production of charcoal. Alder, willow or black dogwood in 3 to 4 ft lengths were stacked as shown (right, above), then covered with straw or ferns kept in position by earth or sand to retain the heat and control air intake. The results of such firing were uneven. About 1830 this method was replaced by horizontal iron cylinders into which the wood was stacked, in a way similar to modern coking methods; the resulting acid liquor byproduct was collected in casks and the gas allowed to escape to assist the firing.

The Gunpowder Factory before 1872, viewed from the bridge over the Lee Navigation. The buildings from the left to the centre were originally part of the saltpetre refinery; after 1872 they were used for the production of guncotton, and turned out 250 tons per year.

These two women are removing impurities from cotton to be used in the manufacture of guncotton, *c.* 1899. Guncotton was made by the action of a mixture of sulphuric and nitric acids on the cotton. This was known as nitration. In the early days explosions were frequent.

The saltpetre refinery, 1895. The saltpetre, which came from Sind, India, is here being purified. On the right is Mr Knowler, the 'father of the factory', with forty-three years service.

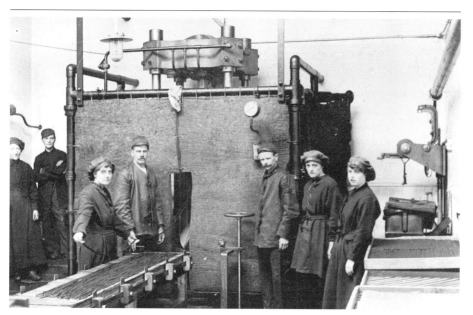

The extrusion of cordite by means of a Tangye press, *c.* 1899. In case of explosion the workers were protected by a thick curtain or a rope mat.

A group of machines used for making 3 in rifle presses or cartridge cases for small arms, *c.* 1917. All the workers are female.

The pressing and moulding room. The press on the right was probably for the hydraulic moulding of guncotton slabs. The assembly on the left appears similar to that in the picture below. The barrels at the front may have held damp guncotton.

After nitration the guncotton was unstable, so excess acid was removed by thorough washing. The date on the machinery is 1899; the photograph was taken *c.* 1917.

Possibly another part of the guncotton production.

Drums being transported by barge, *c.* 1895. These are thought to contain acetone which was first used in the manufacture of cordite in 1889. The forest of trees behind the barge have all been coppiced, presumably to provide wood for charcoal production.

A delightful picture showing what the well-dressed lady munition worker was wearing, *c*. 1917.

This man is wearing danger clothing, *c*. 1899. Notice the footwear which shows a flat combined sole and heel, to negate the risk of sparking from nail-heads.

Not a Western-style hold-up! One of the establishment police checks a worker for matches and tobacco before he enters the factory gate in Powder Mill Lane in 1895. When the nearby river was dredged in 1960, a large number of clay pipes was found where they had been discarded by the workers.

These dogs with their handlers form a deterrent to trespassers. This photograph was taken after the Royal Gunpowder Factory closed and the site had become a government research establishment.

This engine, one of four bought in 1917, had a 10 hp single-cylinder water-cooled engine; it was started on petrol and then ran on the less dangerous paraffin.

Explosives were transferred by rail in the 1850s but mechanical haulage started in 1916. This truck was powered by Edison storage batteries; note the battery box. One such truck still survives.

A barge like this would have been used to transfer materials made at Waltham to Woolwich.

A busy scene, 1899. The bridge is raised, the boats are loaded and ready to go down river.

This explosion of 1843 claimed seven lives. The blast wall on the right proved inadequate. Michael Faraday was brought into the resultant enquiry as a consultant.

The funeral at the Abbey Church of the men killed in the 1843 explosion. In some cases weighted coffins were used to conceal the absence of a body.

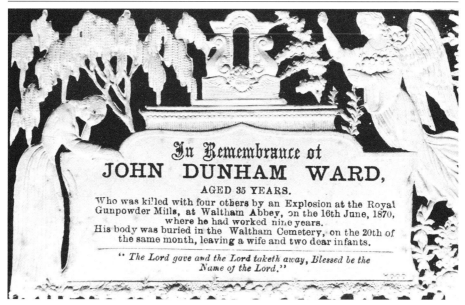

A memorial card issued after a later explosion of 1870. One of the 'two dear infants' is Phoebe Ward (see p. 75).

The last of the gunpowder 'incorporating mills', the result of neglect not explosion; incorporation was a process of intimately mixing the loosely mixed 'green charge' by crushing and grinding; a mill-cake was the result. This mill was destroyed in the late 1950s because of contamination. The last functioning mill had been put out of action by a bomb in 1941.

The boiler house gang. Four of the men have head coverings for protection when carrying coal. Two others have large shovels, which leaves the foreman and chargehand in their bowler hats.

PIONEER OF CORDITE MANUFACTUR
AT WALTHAM ABBEY.
1891.

A group of cordite workers. The first charge of cordite is said to have been nitrated on 16 March 1891. On 7 May 1894 an explosion in this part of the factory killed four men and injured twenty more.

Except for two water wheels at Three Mill, Stratford, this is the only surviving water wheel driven by the River Lea. This wheel is beside a single-storey brick building which retains its mid-nineteenth-century water-driven hydraulic pump.

Early factory fire service. Little is known about this trio except that they are obviously determined to deal with any fire in sight!

The aftermath of an explosion on 21 October 1890 in the incorporating mills. This photograph shows iron runners or rollers and the overturned drenching pan above. Iron runners superseded stone wheels, as they could be smaller and were safer.

The cleaning gang at the turn of the century. Once the gunpowder ingredients have been mixed the powder or 'green charge' is explosive. The danger is minimized by sweeping up and cleaning with wet mops.

OUT AND ABOUT

Waltham Abbey is thirteen miles north of London on the Greenwich meridian, yet the town retains much of its rural character. The Abbey Church is the focus of the town with the grounds and meadows to the north being much as they were in medieval times. To the south-east is Epping Forest, the remains of the ancient forest of Waltham. The forest forms a barrier between Waltham and the rest of Essex. The principal link to north and south would have been via Waltham Cross in Hertfordshire; trams, trolley buses and trains continued the tradition.

Many of the hamlets and villages around Waltham-Upshire, High Beech, Holyfield, Nazeing and Sewardstone, retain a number of their old farms and cottages and some of their individual village atmosphere.

Today the meadows on each side of the river are part of the Lee Valley Regional Park. Old gravel workings have been developed into sanctuaries for birds, and scrapes have been formed for waders. The Cornmill meadows are a haven for dragonflies. The M25 motorway runs to the south of the town with access a mile and half from the town centre.

One mile west of Waltham Abbey is the town of Waltham Cross in Hertfordshire. The name is derived from the Eleanor Cross shown here, viewed from the north-west. Queen Eleanor, wife of Edward I, died at Harby in Nottinghamshire in November 1290. Her body was carried to Westminster Abbey by road, and a cross was erected to mark the resting place at the end of each day's journey. Waltham Cross is one of the three ancient ones which survive.

The construction of the crosses was supervised by John de Bello. The figures of the queen and the other sculptures were the work of the London goldsmith William Torel. Notice the posting house sign of the Falcon Hotel spanning the roadway. In 1617 this inn was known as the Roebuck. The road to the right leads to Enfield and London, that on the left is to Waltham Abbey along a causeway across the marshes.

A tram at the terminus of the metropolitan tramway network which reached Waltham Cross in 1904. Notice the Eleanor Cross in the background and Ye Olde Foure Swannes.

A charabanc, outside the Roman Urn public house in Cheshunt, c. 1925. This was the standard mode of transport for excursions.

Waltham Cross station looking north towards the road bridge, *c.* 1905. The line from Liverpool Street to Broxbourne was opened on 15 September 1840 as the North and Eastern Railway. When this picture was taken the line was part of the Great Eastern Railway. A level crossing preceded the bridge.

Another view of the station, with maintenance work under way, looking south towards London when the platform was on the north side of the road bridge. The platform was moved to its present location in about 1890.

Horse-drawn barges were a common sight on the Lee Navigation. This photograph shows the last barge horse, and the lock-keeper, at Waltham Common lock in the 1970s. The owner of this horse was Mr Green of Holloway, who reckoned to travel thirty miles a day. Note the pollarded trees.

The old Abbey Farmhouse pictured from the north-west across the Cornmill stream. In about 1700 this was the stable block, with accommodation over, belonging to Sir Anthony Denny of Abbey House (see p. 65). It survived as a farmhouse until 1935.

The wheat harvest at Monkhams Field between the two world wars.

The junction of Farm Hill Road, Honey Lane and Broomstick Hall Road, 1889. The timber building is the old Green Man with the present public house nearing completion behind it. In the distance on the right are timber-framed cottages still standing and dating from about 1800.

The Round House in Crooked Mile, built about 1825 as a lodge to Monkhams and formerly known as Eagle Lodge. The estate was broken up in about 1950 and the eagles and gates disappeared; the house is still occupied.

The lodge to Upshire Hall in Honey Lane; it dates from *c.* 1810. The route of the M25 ran through the estate, but as a listed building the lodge was dismantled and rebuilt on the other side of the motorway.

St Thomas' Church, Upshire, built in 1902 by John Bentley (see p. 77). Sir Thomas Buxton of nearby Warlies (see p. 120) met the cost.

All Saints' Church, Nazeing, about four and a half miles north-north-east of Waltham. In 1631–2 the Revd John Eliot and others set out from Nazeing for the New World.

Upshire school. In 1853, Miss Banbury of Warlies gave land for a school in the village; Sir Thomas Buxton paid for the building. It was transferred to the Waltham School Board in 1877. In 1939 it was replaced by a new school.

Sewardstone school, with places for a hundred pupils, was built by the Waltham School Board in 1874. Between the wars numbers declined and it was closed in 1939. The village hall now stands on the site in Dawes Hill.

Holy Innocents Church, High Beech, opened 1873, consecrated 1883. In 1836 the parish of High Beech was formed from part of Waltham Holy Cross and a church (St Paul's) was built at the bottom of the hill in Church Road. By 1842 it had fallen into disrepair caused by damp and this second church was built.

A coal tax post. After the Fire of London in 1666, a tax was levied on coal coming into the city and the money was devoted to rebuilding. The duty was finally abolished in 1890.

Duke of Wellington inn at High Beech, with the two lady Proprietors at the door and a Character called Pipey the Hermit

The Duke of Wellington inn, High Beech, not far from Dick Turpin's cave (see below). The pub still attracts a good trade from visitors to Epping Forest.

The public house called Turpin's Cave. Whether the site was ever used by the highwayman it is impossible to say, but this was one of the attractions after Epping Forest was opened to the public by Queen Victoria in 1882.

The south front of Warlies, Upshire, *c.* 1900. From about 1730, Richard Morgan began to enlarge what had been a small estate and by 1749 it had reached its present size. In 1787 it was bought by Walter Urquart who decided to modernize the house; the façade in the picture dates from 1788. He sold the estate in 1801 and in 1851 it came to Sir Edward North Buxton, 2nd baronet, who needed a seat in Essex to get him into Parliament.

Sir Thomas Fowell Buxton, 3rd baronet, 1837–1915, the eldest son of Edward. He was a philanthropist whose interests included: the family brewery of Truman, Hanbury and Buxton; social problems in the East End; the Tower Hamlets Volunteers; the Anti-Slavery Society; and the Commons and Footpath Preservation Society. He was high sheriff and deputy lieutenant of Essex. From 1895 to 1898 he was governor of South Australia but was compelled to return because of his wife's (Lady Victoria's) ill health. One of his favourite mottoes was 'When in doubt, do the enterprising thing'!

The monogram TFB of Thomas Fowell Buxton on the 1879 north wing at Warlies. Note the open hand indicating the baronetcy.

The carving over the entrance under the portico of 1788 at Warlies (see p. 119).

Two interiors of Warlies. Above, the sitting room, 1894. Below, originally the drawing room in 1862 but later the library.

These two obelisks are situated on the Warlies estate and could be seen from the house. The first has the name of Obelisk Farm attached and was originally covered in stucco; the other may also have been so covered.

Local legend, without any foundation, says the former obelisk marks the spot where Boudicca, Queen of the Iceni, took poison after her defeat by the Romans at the nearby Iron Age camp of Ambersbury Banks, and the latter is said to show where she died.

Copped Hall, *c.* 1908. The ruin of this once fine building lies about three miles north-east of Waltham Abbey and is clearly visible from the M25. This photograph shows the third Copped Hall; the previous two had occupied a site 300 yd to the north-west. The Fitz Aucher family, who served the king as royal huntsmen of the great forest, held the first hall from *c.* 1150 to 1337. From 1350 to 1537 it was held by the Abbots of Waltham and in 1537 it was surrendered to King Henry VIII. Mary Tudor lived here during the reign of Edward VI and in 1564 the estate was granted by Queen Elizabeth to Sir Thomas Heneage. He built the second hall as a 'noble large house with a court in the middle'. This stood for nearly 200 years until the present hall was built in 1751–8. At the end of the nineteenth century it was extended and the gardens developed. It was destroyed by fire on 5 May 1917, and all that remains is a shell.

The magnificent ornamental Italian gardens at Copped Hall were designed with grand walled terraces, fountains and statues. The parterres and geometric patterns of the gardens were laid out in the nineteenth century.

Acknowledgements

This book has been compiled by Janet Grove, Ted Ayres, Cliff Gould and Jack Littlefair, all members of the Waltham Abbey Historical Society, and edited by the Society's President Dr Ken Bascombe.

More than 90 per cent of the photographs are from the collection of the Society which was started by the late Sidney Puddephatt. The editor thanks the Epping Forest District Museum for permission to select items from their collection. Thanks are also due to the following for allowing the use of their photographs: The Marquess of Salisbury (for the map on p. 10), Aerofilms (for the front cover picture), G.W.C. Taylor, Doug Lewis, Cliff Gould, Jack Littlefair and the Waltham Abbey Salvation Army. Technical advice on Section Six was given by Malcolm McLaren, Ron Holt, Alf Nicholls, Arthur Witham, Kim Henshaw, Diane Howse and Bryan Howard.

BRITAIN IN OLD PHOTOGRAPHS

To order any of these titles please telephone Littlehampton Book Services on 01903 721596

Scunthorpe, *D Taylor*
Skegness, *W Kime*
Around Skegness, *W Kime*

LONDON

Balham and Tooting, *P Loobey*
Crystal Palace, Penge & Anerley, *M Scott*
Greenwich and Woolwich, *K Clark*
Hackney: A Second Selection, *D Mander*
Lewisham and Deptford, *J Coulter*
Lewisham and Deptford: A Second Selection, *J Coulter*
Streatham, *P Loobey*
Around Whetstone and North Finchley, *J Heathfield*
Woolwich, *B Evans*

MONMOUTHSHIRE

Chepstow and the River Wye, *A Rainsbury*
Monmouth and the River Wye, *Monmouth Museum*

NORFOLK

Great Yarmouth, *M Teun*
Norwich, *M Colman*
Wymondham and Attleborough, *P Yaxley*

NORTHAMPTONSHIRE

Around Stony Stratford, *A Lambert*

NOTTINGHAMSHIRE

Arnold and Bestwood, *M Spick*
Arnold and Bestwood: A Second Selection, *M Spick*
Changing Face of Nottingham, *G Oldfield*
Mansfield, *Old Mansfield Society*
Around Newark, *T Warner*
Nottingham: 1944–1974, *D Whitworth*
Sherwood Forest, *D Ottewell*
Victorian Nottingham, *M Payne*

OXFORDSHIRE

Around Abingdon, *P Horn*
Banburyshire, *M Barnett & S Gosling*
Burford, *A Jewell*
Around Didcot and the Hagbournes, *B Lingham*
Garsington, *M Gunther*
Around Henley-on-Thames, *S Ellis*
Oxford: The University, *J Rhodes*
Thame to Watlington, *N Hood*
Around Wallingford, *D Beasley*
Witney, *T Worley*
Around Witney, *C Mitchell*
Witney District, *T Worley*
Around Woodstock, *J Bond*

POWYS

Brecon, *Brecknock Museum*
Welshpool, *E Bredsdorff*

SHROPSHIRE

Shrewsbury, *D Trumper*
Whitchurch to Market Drayton, *M Morris*

SOMERSET

Bath, *J Hudson*
Bridgwater and the River Parrett, *R Fitzhugh*
Bristol, *D Moorcroft & N Campbell-Sharp*
Changing Face of Keynsham,
  B Lowe & M Whitehead

Chard and Ilminster, *G Gosling & F Huddy*
Crewkerne and the Ham Stone Villages,
  G Gosling & F Huddy
Around Keynsham and Saltford, *B Lowe & T Brown*
Midsomer Norton and Radstock, *C Howell*
Somerton, Ilchester and Langport, *G Gosling & F Huddy*
Taunton, *N Chipchase*
Around Taunton, *N Chipchase*
Wells, *C Howell*
Weston-Super-Mare, *S Poole*
Around Weston-Super-Mare, *S Poole*
West Somerset Villages, *K Houghton & E Thomas*

STAFFORDSHIRE

Aldridge, *J Farrow*
Bilston, *E Rees*
Black Country Transport: Aviation, *A Brew*
Around Burton upon Trent, *G Sowerby & R Farman*
Bushbury, *A Chatwin, M Mills & E Rees*
Around Cannock, *M Mills & S Belcher*
Around Leek, *R Poole*
Lichfield, *H Clayton & K Simmons*
Around Pattingham and Wombourne, *M Griffiths,*
  P Leigh & M Mills
Around Rugeley, *T Randall & J Anslow*
Smethwick, *J Maddison*
Stafford, *J Anslow & T Randall*
Around Stafford, *J Anslow & T Randall*
Stoke-on-Trent, *I Lawley*
Around Tamworth, *R Sulima*
Around Tettenhall and Codsall, *M Mills*
Tipton, Wednesbury and Darlaston, *R Pearson*
Walsall, *M Gilbert & M Lewis*
Wednesbury, *I Bott*
West Bromwich, *R Pearson*

SUFFOLK

Ipswich: A Second Selection, *D Kindred*
Around Ipswich, *D Kindred*
Around Mildenhall, *C Dring*
Southwold to Aldeburgh, *H Phelps*
Around Woodbridge, *H Phelps*

SURREY

Cheam and Belmont, *P Berry*
Croydon, *S Bligh*
Dorking and District, *K Harding*
Around Dorking, *A Jackson*
Around Epsom, *P Berry*
Farnham: A Second Selection, *J Parratt*
Around Haslemere and Hindhead, *T Winter & G Collyer*
Richmond, *Richmond Local History Society*
Sutton, *P Berry*

SUSSEX

Arundel and the Arun Valley, *J Godfrey*
Bishopstone and Seaford, *P Pople & P Berry*
Brighton and Hove, *J Middleton*
Brighton and Hove: A Second Selection, *J Middleton*
Around Crawley, *M Goldsmith*
Hastings, *P Haines*
Hastings: A Second Selection, *P Haines*
Around Haywards Heath, *J Middleton*
Around Heathfield, *A Gillet & B Russell*
Around Heathfield: A Second Selection,
  A Gillet & B Russell
High Weald, *B Harwood*
High Weald: A Second Selection, *B Harwood*
Horsham and District, *T Wales*

Lewes, *J Middleton*
RAF Tangmere, *A Saunders*
Around Rye, *A Dickinson*
Around Worthing, *S White*

WARWICKSHIRE

Along the Avon from Stratford to Tewkesbury, *J Jeremiah*
Bedworth, *J Burton*
Coventry, *D McGrory*
Around Coventry, *D McGrory*
Nuneaton, *S Clews & S Vaughan*
Around Royal Leamington Spa, *J Cameron*
Around Royal Leamington Spa: A Second Selection,
  J Cameron
Around Warwick, *R Booth*

WESTMORLAND

Eden Valley, *J Marsh*
Kendal, *M & P Duff*
South Westmorland Villages, *J Marsh*
Westmorland Lakes, *J Marsh*

WILTSHIRE

Around Amesbury, *P Daniels*
Chippenham and Lacock, *A Wilson & M Wilson*
Around Corsham and Box, *A Wilson & M Wilson*
Around Devizes, *D Buxton*
Around Highworth, *G Tanner*
Around Highworth and Faringdon, *G Tanner*
Around Malmesbury, *A Wilson*
Marlborough: A Second Selection, *P Colman*
Around Melksham,
  Melksham and District Historical Association
Nadder Valley, *R. Sawyer*
Salisbury, *P Saunders*
Salisbury: A Second Selection, *P Daniels*
Salisbury: A Third Selection, *P Daniels*
Around Salisbury, *P Daniels*
Swindon: A Third Selection, *The Swindon Society*
Swindon: A Fourth Selection, *The Swindon Society*
Trowbridge, *M Marshman*
Around Wilton, *P Daniels*
Around Wootton Bassett, Cricklade and Purton, *T Sharp*

WORCESTERSHIRE

Evesham to Bredon, *F Archer*
Around Malvern, *K Smith*
Around Pershore, *M Dowty*
Redditch and the Needle District, *R Saunders*
Redditch: A Second Selection, *R Saunders*
Around Tenbury Wells, *D Green*
Worcester, *M Dowty*
Around Worcester, *R Jones*
Worcester in a Day, *M Dowty*
Worcestershire at Work, *R Jones*

YORKSHIRE

Huddersfield: A Second Selection, *H Wheeler*
Huddersfield: A Third Selection, *H Wheeler*
Leeds Road and Rail, *R Vickers*
Pontefract, *R van Riel*
Scarborough, *D Coggins*
Scarborough's War Years, *R Percy*
Skipton and the Dales, *Friends of the Craven Museum*
Around Skipton-in-Craven, *Friends of the Craven Museum*
Yorkshire Wolds, *I & M Sumner*